Black Canadians • Achievement

OUT

of the

PAST

INTO

the

FUTURE

Written by Robert Ffrench

Illustrated by Henry V. Bishop

PRIDE

COMMUNICATIONS

"If you see truth" and "We are the future" from *If You See Truth/Poems for Children and Young People* By Lillian Allen. Toronto: Verse to Vinyl, 1990. Copyright 1990 by Lillian Allen. Reprinted by permission of Well Versed Publications.

"The Profile of Africa" and "When Black and White See Eye to Eye" from *Save the World for Me*. By Maxine Tynes. Lawrencetown Beach, N.S.: Pottersfield Press, 1991. Copyright 1991 by Maxine Tynes. Reprinted by permission of the author.

Activity on page adapted from *Color Me Light of the World*. By Sharon N. Carter. Chicago: African American Images, 1989.

PRIDE Communications
P.O. Box 28058
Dartmouth, Nova Scotia, Canada
B2W 6E2
Tel: (902) 827–4827

This publication was made possible through the financial contribution of the
Nova Scotia Department of Supply and Services

Editor Susan Lucy

Graphic Design and Activities Illustration Elaine Frampton

Filmmaker Nova Scotia Digital Technologies Inc.

Printed by McCurdy Printing and Typesetting Ltd.

Distributed by Umbrella Press
          56 Rivercourt Boulevard
          Toronto, Ontario
          M4J 3A4
          Tel: (416) 696–6665
          Fax: (416) 696–9189

Printed on paper that
contains recycled fibre

Canadian Cataloging in Publication Data

Ffrench, Robert, 1959-

    Black Canadian achievement

    (Black Canadian)
    Includes bibliographical references.
    ISBN 0-9698350-0-0

1. Blacks -- Canada -- History -- Juvenile
literature. 2. Blacks -- Canada -- Biography --
Juvenile literature. 3. Blacks -- Canada -- History
-- Problems, exercises, etc. -- Juvenile literature.
4. Blacks -- Canada -- Biography -- Problems,
exercises, etc. -- Juvenile literature. I. Title.
II. Series: Ffrench, Robert, 1959-   . Black
Canadian.

FC106.N3F44 1994   971'.004'96   C94-950133-6
F1035.N3F44 1994

Contents

DEDICATION

This book is dedicated to my parents, to my wife Regina, to my sons Andy, Adrian, and Luke, and also in loving memory of my oldest brother Silas, who as a teacher believed in the value of education for everyone.

Henry V. Bishop

To my parents and friends who believed in this project, thank you. For my children, Whitney and Ellis, may you always believe in yourself and seek the truth. Accept the past and recognize the future is yours.

Love always
Robert Ffrench

ACKNOWLEDGEMENTS

This book began as a personal journey and exploration into an area that in the most part was hidden throughout most of our lives and, in particular, the lives of our young people.

Many people took the time to assist in the development of the book, never asking for anything in return. All those involved share a view that knowledge is a key to overcoming the fear and distrust some in our society have towards others.

We wish to acknowledge the contribution and assistance of Doris Evans, Nancy Sparks, Ken Pearson, Cindy Hilchey, Robert Upshaw, Allison Lannan, Vanroy Tolbitt, Shirley Sangster, Adrienne Hopper, Earl Clyke, Cathy Ross, Dan Sargeant, Pat Johnson, and Carolyn Banfield.

Preface

Canadians of African descent are known as either African Canadians or Black Canadians. It makes no difference if they were born in Canada, the Caribbean, or any other part of the world. To be called African Canadian recognizes a proud heritage and history. This book will use both terms, African and Black, in describing the people.

Introduction

No study of our Canadian history can be complete without acknowledging the roles and contributions Black Canadians have made over many years.

Through slavery, oppression, racism, and forced movement, African Canadians have continued to make progress in the hope for equality.

Canadian school texts and teaching information are admittedly lacking, and what is available tends to be designed for older age groups—beyond the time when images have had their most damaging effect.

It is our hope that learning about the exploits and achievements of Black Canadians in ways that are fun can promote a greater understanding and develop positive relationships between students of all backgrounds.

The intent of this book is to provide study areas that will stimulate the minds of the young to dig deeper and explore for even more information. Individuals have been highlighted for the long-term effect their efforts have had on Black Canadians. Many others have played equally prominent roles, and we respectfully honour their contributions.

Beginnings

No matter how they came to this country, all Black Canadians have ancestors who came from Africa. Africa is a continent of many different people and cultures. It has a rich and important history as the birthplace of civilization.

Akhenaton, Pharaoh of Egypt (1375–1358 BC)

Akhenaton (Ak hen a tun) was the first Egyptian ruler to believe in the idea of one god. He taught a doctrine of peace and love. He and his wife Queen Nefretiti changed Egyptian culture so much that their influence was felt centuries later.

Sunni Ali Ber, King of Songhay (1464–1492)

Sunni Ali Ber (Soo ni Al ee Burr) was king of what is today Nigeria and ruled for 28 years. During that time his country grew into the largest, most powerful empire in West Africa. He built a great army of soldiers, including a horse and camel cavalry with men in armour. He was called Ali the Great by his people.

Affonso I, King of the Kongo (1506–1540)

Affonso I (Af fon so) ruled an empire in the area that today is Cameroon, Congo, Gabon, and the Central African Republic. He saw his country not as a group of separate cultures, but as a unified nation. He was the first Black ruler to resist the slave trade.

Queen Amina of Zaria (*ca* 1588)

Queen Amina (A mee nah) ruled over what now is Benin and Nigeria around 1588. She was the elder daughter of Bakwa Turunku who founded the Zazzau kingdom in 1536. Amina is generally remembered for her fierce military exploits. She lead her army into many wars and was never defeated. Considered a brilliant leader, Amina erected great walled camps and is credited with building the famous Zaria wall.

Activity 1: Discover a Continent

To discover the hidden continent, shade in the correct area of each square. Follow the shading code and the example given to you (2C).

Additional questions found on page 56.

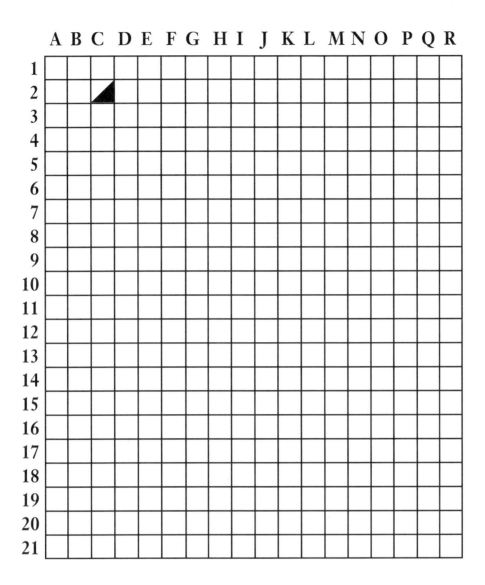

Grid columns: A B C D E F G H I J K L M N O P Q R
Grid rows: 1 through 21

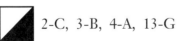

 2-C, 3-B, 4-A, 13-G

 10-Q, 11-P, 12-O, 15-O, 16-N, 19-M, 21-L

 1-K, 3-N, 4-O, 13-O

7-A, 8-B, 9-F, 11-G, 17-G, 19-H, 21-I

 1-E, 2-D, 2-K, 3-L, 3-M, 5-A, 5-O, 6-A, 6-O, 7-O, 8-C, 8-D, 8-E, 8-O, 9-P, 9-Q, 10-G, 12-H, 14-G, 14-O, 15-G, 16-G, 17-M, 18-H, 18-M, 20-I, 20-L, 21-J, 21-K

When you complete all the squares, you will see the outline of the continent called _ _ _ _ _ _ .
To finish the map, shade the inside area green for the land and the outside area blue for the ocean.

3

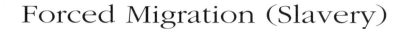

Forced Migration (Slavery)

A slave is a human being who is treated as property by another person. The first records of slave-owning people go back to the Athenians of ancient Greece. They travelled north into what is now Europe to conquer those lands and take prisoners. Many of those conquered were Slavic in origin. The word "slave" comes from the same word as "Slavic" and was used to identify the hostages.

One of the worst examples of slavery was that of the Africans captured to be transported and sold in the New World. Millions of people were taken from their homes and used as hostage workers throughout Canada, the United States, and the Caribbean.

Oftentimes those captured were the best and brightest of the people. Kings and queens were among those who were put in chains and had their rights taken away. Families were separated, never to see each other again. A proud people were treated worse than animals. While the slave owners may have kept their bodies in chains, the people never gave up hope and remained determined to be free.

Many of the first Blacks to settle in Canada were brought as slaves. Others came at a later time when slavery was no longer legal in this country.

Activity 2: Hieroglyphics
A kind of picture writing called hieroglyphics was created by the great African civilization of ancient Egypt. There were more than 700 different signs called hieroglyphs, each representing a sound, an object, or an idea. Here are some hieroglyphs that you can use as a code, swapping the hieroglyph for a letter in English.

Additional questions found on page 56.

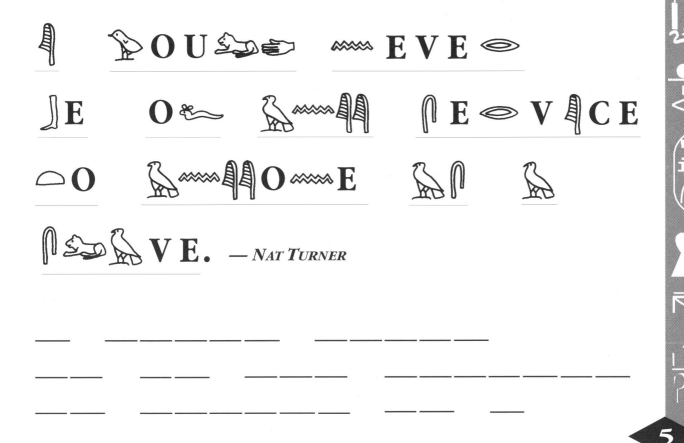

A vulture	**B** leg	**D** hand	**F** viper	**G** stand	**H** rope	**I** reed
J serpent	**K** basket	**L** lion	**M** owl	**N** water	**P** stool	**Q** hill
R mouth	**S** cloth	**T** loaf	**W** chick	**Y** reeds	**Z** bolt	

Can you translate the passage below from picture writing to modern writing?
There are no hieroglyphs for some letters, like E and O, so they have been written in.

I WOUL D NEVE R

BE OF ANY SERVICE

TO ANYONE AS A

SLAVE. — *Nat Turner*

___ _____ _____

___ __ ___ _____

___ _____ __ _ __

_____ .

Settlement

The history of Blacks in Canada reaches back to the beginnings of our country. There were important periods of Black settlement in Canada. Each has had a long-lasting effect on the country and Blacks alike.

Mattieu da Costa (ca 1605)

Mattieu da Costa was the first-known Black to arrive on Canadian soil. He came with an expedition led by Pierre de Gua, Sieur de Monts, who founded the colony of Port Royal in what is now Nova Scotia in 1605. Da Costa served as interpreter between the French and the Mi'kmaq who lived nearby. The involvement of da Costa in early trade was vital in the colony's attempt to adapt to the New World.

Activity 3: TV Interview

Choose a partner. Imagine that one of you is the first person of African descent to go to Canada. The other is a reporter for a television news program who is interviewing that person about their trip. Here are some questions that might be asked during the interview. Can you think of any others?

TV INTERVIEW

1. What is your name ?

_____

_____

2. Why did you go to Canada ?

_____

_____

_____

_____

3. Where did you come from ? _____

_____

4. How did you get to Canada ? _____

_____

5. Where in Canada did you first go ? _____

_____

6. _____

_____

7. _____

_____

8. _____

_____

9. _____

_____

10. _____

_____

7

Black Loyalists

An important group to come to Canada were the Black Loyalists. In 1775 the thirteen American Colonies rebelled against the government of Great Britain. Many people who lived in the colonies did not want to join the rebels. These people, who were known as the United Empire Loyalists, began to leave the breakaway colonies and move north. The British government encouraged the Loyalists and offered to free any African hostages, referred to as slaves, who would join their forces. Many slaves and their owners responded quickly.

As word spread, thousands of slaves risked their lives and tried to escape. Some made their way to Canada by walking, while others were taken aboard British ships when the war was over. Approximately 10 per cent of the Loyalists who reached Nova Scotia were Black.

The Maroons

Another group of people of African descent who left their mark on the early beginnings of Canada were called Maroons and came from the island of Jamaica. Jamaica was an important British colony in the West Indies. The Maroons were escaped slaves who from 1655 guarded their freedom in the mountains of Jamaica. For over 100 years they fought off all efforts to recapture them.

Some of those fierce freedom fighters were tricked by the British and were sent to Nova Scotia. A group of approximately 600 arrived in Halifax in 1796 aboard three small ships: the *Dover*, the *Mary*, and the *Ann*. The Maroons played a key role in the defence of Halifax by building the Maroon Bastion on Citadel Hill. They also formed their own militia unit, which was natural as they were all very skilled fighters.

As a direct result of racism, they experienced many problems and became increasingly uncomfortable in Nova Scotia. About 500 Maroons asked for and received permission to leave Nova Scotia and settle in Sierra Leone, a British colony in Africa. They travelled aboard a ship called the *Asia* in 1800 to begin a new life there.

War of 1812

In 1812 the British colonies of Canada and the newly formed United States of America went to war. There were many African Canadians who fought for the British. Captain Runchey's Company of Coloured Men was a special segregated (all-Black) unit that took part in many battles, including the famous Battle of Queenston Heights.

After the war ended, approximately 2,000 Black refugees came to Canada wishing to escape slavery. Many of them settled and lived in Nova Scotia and New Brunswick.

The Profile of Africa

we wear our skin like a fine fabric
we people of colour
brown, black, tan coffeecoffee cream ebony
beautiful, strong, exotic in profile
flowering lips
silhouette obsidian planes, curves, structure
like a many- shaded mosaic
we wear our skin like a flag
we share our colour like a blanket
we cast our skin like a shadow
we wear our skin like a map
chart my beginning by my profile
chart my beginning by my colour
read the map of my heritage in
my face
my skin
the dark flash of eye
the profile of Africa.

—*Maxine Tynes*

9

Escape from Slavery

Slavery ended in Canada in 1834. Even before that, slavery was gradually ending. In 1793 a law made it illegal to bring slaves into Upper Canada (Ontario). Slaves learned that if they reached this country, Canada would refuse to send them back to the United States.

The third large early movement of Blacks into Canada occurred when escaped slaves made their way north from the United States. Around the time just before the American Civil War (1861–65), this movement reached its largest numbers. Canada was believed to be the land of freedom. But, the road to freedom was dangerous, and many who tried failed. Even the punishments they would have to suffer if caught did not stop thousands from trying to escape (over 30,000 reached Canada). Some of those that did make the journey often returned to assist others along what was to become known as the "Underground Railroad." Risking their own lives, these brave people tried to help as many other slaves to freedom as they could.

Activity 4: Escaped Slaves—Equipment

Imagine that you are an escaped slave trying to get to Canada. You have only enough room for 10 things to help you through the cold winter coming. What will you bring with you? (Remember you have to carry everything.)

Item	Why would you take it?

1. _____ _____

2. _____ _____

3. _____ _____

4. _____ _____

5. _____ _____

6. _____ _____

7. _____ _____

8. _____ _____

9. _____ _____

10. _____ _____

William Hall (1829-1904)

William Hall joined the Royal Navy when he was just 12 years old. He was a sailor for 26 years and in 1857 became the first Canadian sailor and also the first Black to win the Victoria Cross, for bravery in war. It is the highest military honour in the British Commonwealth.

Born in 1826 at Horton Bluff, Kings County, Nova Scotia, Hall was the son of slaves freed when the ship carrying them was captured and released in Halifax. He served on HMS *Victory* and was given medals for actions in the Battle of Inkerman during the Crimean War in 1853 and also the Siege at Sebastopol. He won the Victoria Cross fighting in India where rebels in the Indian Army were attempting to break away from British rule. Hall volunteered to join a gun crew whose job it was to make a hole in the walls that surrounded the City of Lucknow. During the fierce fighting, with most of the others killed or injured, Hall kept the cannon firing until part of the wall finally fell.

Activity 5:
The Victoria Cross •
Design Your Own Medal

This is the Victoria Cross, the medal won by William Hall.

Imagine that a medal has been awarded to you. Design the medal, then write a description of how you won it.

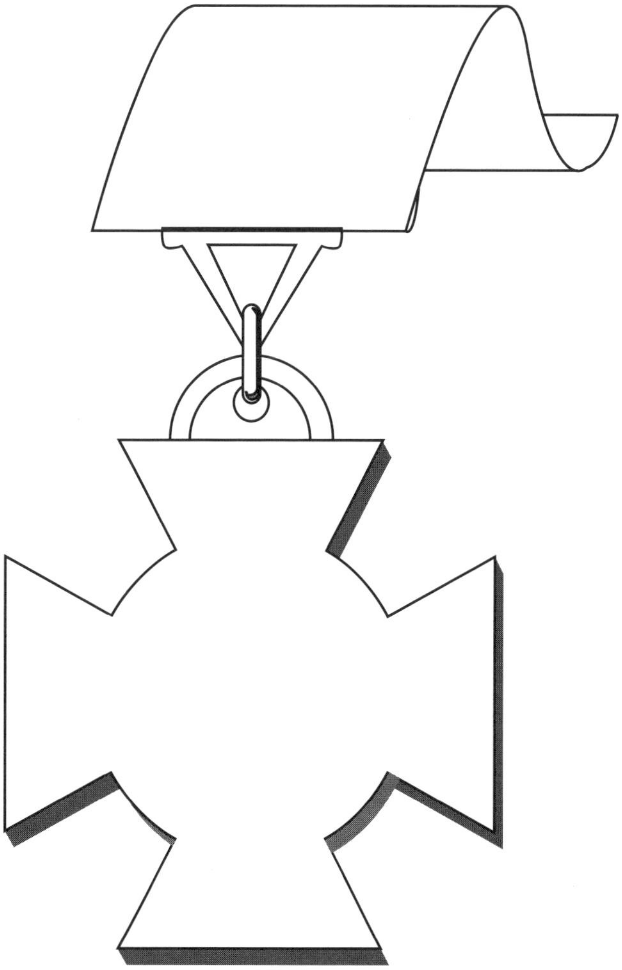

_____

_____

_____

_____

_____

_____

_____

_____

_____

_____

_____

_____

Answer these questions about the Victoria Cross. Ask someone to help you (your parents or your teacher).

1. When was the Victoria Cross first given?_____

2. Who was the Victoria Cross named for? _____

3. How many Canadians have won the Victoria Cross? _____

4. Who gives the medal? _____

5. Can you name the province with Victoria as the capital city?_____

13

Colonel Stephen Bluck (*ca* 1752-1796)

Colonel Stephen Bluck led the Black Pioneers during the American Revolution. The Pioneers were an all-Black regiment of free men and former slaves who fought for the British. After the war like many other Black Loyalists, he came to Nova Scotia and settled in Shelburne around 1783. He became a teacher and one of the leaders of the Nova Scotia Black Loyalists.

No. 2 Construction Battalion C.E.F. (1916-1920)

When the First World War started in 1914 Blacks were not allowed in the military. They kept volunteering and finally were allowed to join, but only in segregated (all-Black) units. The Nova Scotia No. 2 Construction Battalion was one of these units, made up of 650 men (Black women still did not have an opportunity to serve their country). The unit built roads and bridges throughout France during the war. Many of the duties occurred under dangerous conditions with fighting nearby, yet they were never issued weapons. Even though the men suffered abuse and were sometimes physically attacked because of the colour of their skin, they served our country with loyalty and bravery. A monument in Pictou, Nova Scotia unveiled on July 10, 1993 honours their contribution.

14 Activity 6: Name the Ships and Places

Unscramble the letters to find the names of the ships and place names. Then match each name to a sentence. You will find the answers in this book.

1. The <u>S</u> <u>A</u> <u>S</u> <u>I</u> was the ship used by Blacks to travel to Sierra Leone.

   _____ ___ ___ ___

2. The ships that carried the Maroons to Halifax were named <u>V</u> <u>R</u> <u>E</u> <u>O</u> <u>D</u> , <u>R</u> <u>A</u> <u>Y</u> <u>M</u>, and <u>N</u> <u>N</u> <u>A</u>.

   _____ _____

   _____ _____ _____

3. William Hall served on this famous ship: <u>R</u> <u>V</u> <u>I</u> <u>Y</u> <u>C</u> <u>O</u> <u>T</u>

   _____ _____ _____ _____

4. The British government brought the Maroons to <u>L</u> <u>X</u> <u>H</u> <u>A</u> <u>A</u> <u>I</u> <u>F.</u>

   _____ _____ _____

5. William Hall won medals for bravery in battles at <u>K</u> <u>M</u> <u>I</u> <u>N</u> <u>N</u> <u>R</u> <u>E</u> <u>A</u> and <u>B</u> <u>L</u> <u>O</u> <u>O</u> <u>S</u> <u>P</u> <u>L</u> <u>E</u> <u>T</u> <u>A</u>.

   _____ _____ _____

   _____ _____ _____ _____

6. Mattieu da Costa helped establish the colony at <u>R</u> <u>P</u> <u>T</u> <u>O</u>   <u>A</u> <u>Y</u> <u>L</u> <u>O</u> <u>R</u>.

   _____ _____ _____ _____

7. Freetown is the capital of this country where former slaves settled: <u>A</u> <u>E</u> <u>R</u> <u>S</u> <u>I</u> <u>R</u> <u>N</u> <u>E</u> <u>E</u> <u>L</u> <u>O.</u>

   _____ _____ _____ _____ _____

15

Additional questions are found on page 56.

Newspapers

Mary Ann Shadd (1823-1893)

The first woman in North America to become the editor of a newspaper was Mary Ann Shadd. Working out of Chatham, Ontario, she published, edited, and wrote for the *Provincial Freeman*. The paper was well known as it called for an end to slavery in the United States and any other mistreatment of Blacks.

Miss Shadd was also well known as a teacher in Ontario. She ran a private school for Black and white students of all ages. Shadd believed that Blacks would make more progress in society by living among, not apart from other people and that education was the key. She went to the United States to assist the Union (or northern) army in the Civil War that took place from 1861 to 1865 between the slave-owning southern states and the northern states who opposed slavery. She later became a lawyer.

Activity 7: Design Your Own Newspaper

An editor is the person who decides what stories and pictures go into a newspaper. Design the front page of a newspaper for your family or class showing the news of the day. On the facing page is a suggested layout of a front page. Use the grid on page 18 to design your own layout.

Write your paper's name in this space

Write the main story headline on these 2 lines

Write your main story here (write small!)

_Paste a picture or drawing here
and add your caption below_

Short story headline here:

Short story :

Thought for the day:

17

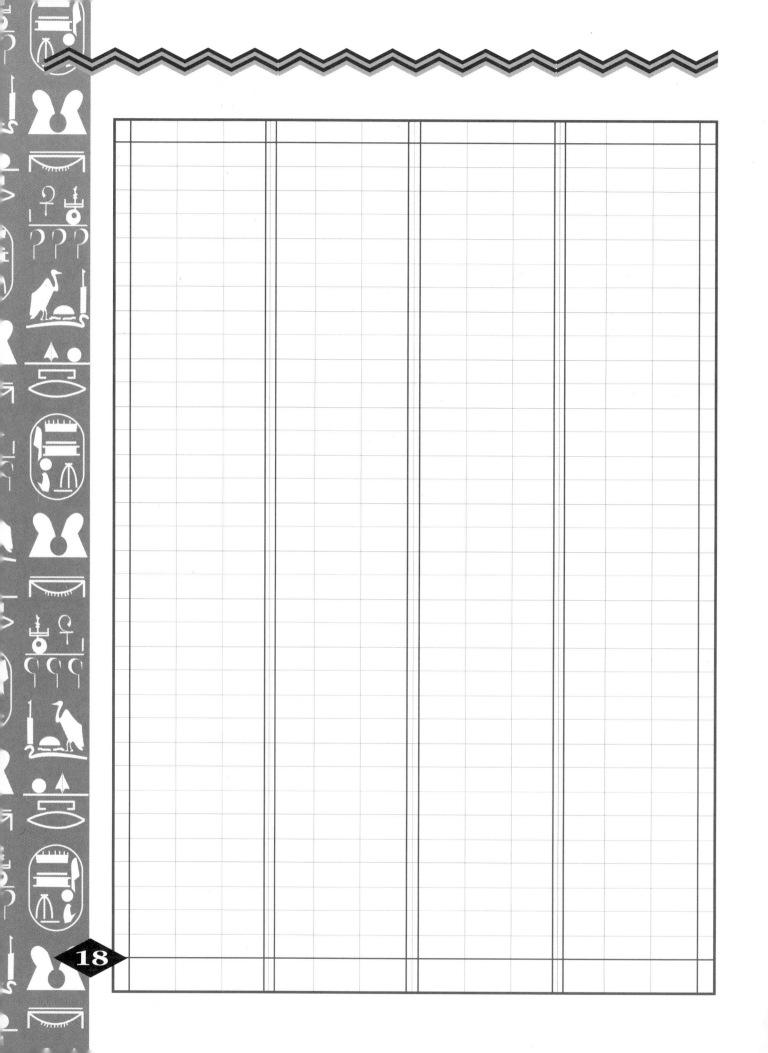

Reverend Samuel Ringgold Ward (*ca* 1817-1866)

Samuel Ringgold Ward began publishing the *Provincial Freeman* on March 25, 1853. Its motto was *"Self-Reliance is the True Road to Independence."* The paper dealt with the problems encountered by refugee Blacks. It raised questions about racial discrimination and urged Blacks to improve themselves by becoming educated and self-reliant. Ward was an excellent speaker who organized branches of the Anti-Slavery Society and gave lectures all over the province of Ontario.

Henry Bibb (1815-1854)

Henry Bibb published *The Voice of the Fugitive* out of Windsor, Ontario. It was aimed at trying to help Blacks who had just escaped slavery in the United States. Bibb was also vocal in his opposition to a separate school system being developed for Black children. He argued that the standard of education for Black children would be lowered. Bibbs' fears were correct, and it took many years to bring about changes that allowed Black and white children to be taught together.

John Ware (1845-1905)

John Ware was a cowboy from Texas who arrived in what is now Alberta in 1882. Born into slavery in the United States, he was set free in 1865. After working as a cowhand for several years, Ware set up his own ranch in the foothills southwest of Calgary. A tall powerful man, Ware was an expert with guns and lassos, but was even more skillful in the handling of cattle and wild horses. He regularly won prize money at early rodeos. Ware wanted to always challenge the toughest animal.

Ware was one of the best-known Blacks to settle in western Canada and won the respect of his fellow ranchers. Many believe he had a role in bringing the first longhorn cattle to Canada. John Ware died in 1905 after the horse he was riding stepped into a hole and fell heavily to the ground, landing on him.

Activity 8:
John Ware Word Search

Find all the words hidden in the puzzle. When you have found all the words, there will be 20 letters left over. Write down the 20 letters in order starting from the top row and going across. When you're finished you will have a message of 6 words.

A T H E K L N C O W B O Y
L R W O O C O H R O P E A
B E S E E S A N O E S A S
E P R A V D S L G J W E E
R X A C X A O A B H I O P
T E L A L E L R L R O R P
A N O T H Y T S O H I R G
G R C T C C L T O Z O R N
A E N L N L I R E L E W I
L T O E A R S F L E A I D
L S R T R E R I T R O L I
O E B E L E K S E D U D R
P W T D E S C A N A D A E

Alberta
black
bronco
Canada
cattle
cowboy
expert
free
gallop
horse
John
lasso
longhorn
power
prize
ranch
riding
rodeo
rope
skill
slave
steer
tall
territories
Texas
Ware
western
wild

1   2   3   4   5   6

7   8   9   10   11   12

13   14   15   16   17   18   19   20

21

Reverend Richard Preston (1790-1861)

Richard Preston became one of the most important church and community leaders in Nova Scotia. Preston escaped slavery and came to Nova Scotia in search of his mother in 1816. He was a leading figure in helping to set up 11 Baptist churches in Nova Scotia and encouraged church members to press for changes that would make their lives easier. Affectionately called "Father Preston" by his congregation, he was trained as a Baptist minister in England and was active in the movement to abolish slavery. One of his greatest accomplishments was the creation of the African United Baptist Association in 1854. Made up of representatives from 12 Black Baptist churches in Nova Scotia, it has grown to become one of the most important Black associations in the history of Nova Scotia.

Activity 9: Stained Glass Window

Colour this stained glass window by matching the colours to the numbers. The message you see is what Richard Preston taught his congregation to have. Why was this message important to him? Additional questions found on page 56.

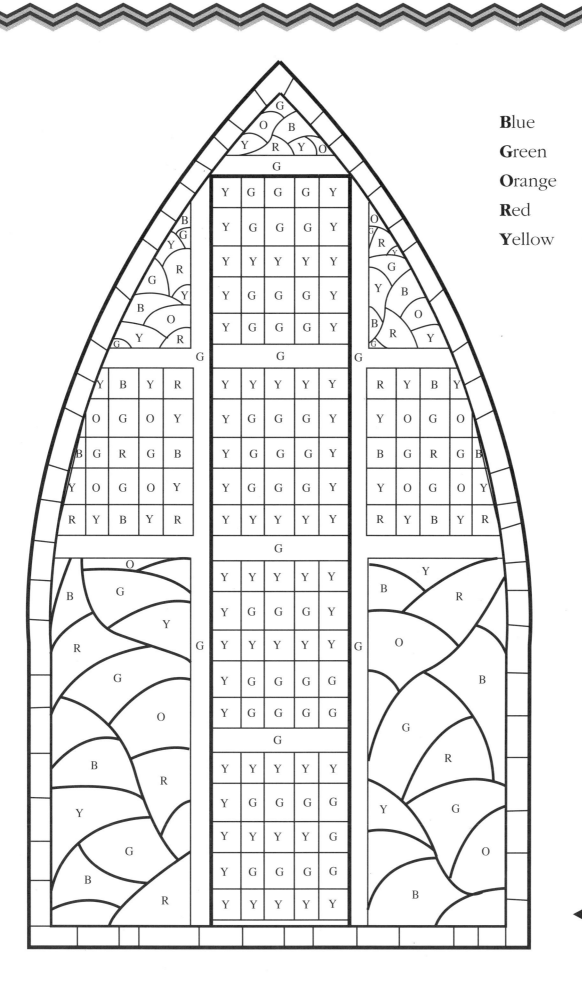

Blue
Green
Orange
Red
Yellow

The Conductors

Harriet Tubman (*ca* 1820-1913)

Harriet Tubman said that she never ran her train off the track and she never lost a passenger. One of the key figures in the Underground Railroad, this "conductor" escaped slavery as a young woman. She came to Canada and settled in St. Catharines, Ontario in 1851. From there she made 19 trips into the United States to help guide more than 300 other slaves to freedom. The first people she helped were her own sister and brothers. At one point rewards of $40,000 were offered to anyone who could capture her.

She was called the Moses of her people, and although she could not read or write was clever enough to outwit her most hostile enemies.

During the American Civil War she even became a nurse and a spy for the Union Army, using her contacts to find and gather information. When that war ended in 1865, and all slaves were freed, the Underground Railroad's work was finished.

Terms

1. The Underground Railroad was not a railroad at all. It was a network of paths and hiding places to help slaves escape north. It began around 1840 and ran until 1860.

2. The conductors were people, Black and white, who led the slaves from one hiding place to another.

3. These hiding places were called "stations."

4. The people who would hide escaped slaves and advise them where to find the next safe station were called "station masters."

5. Persons who gave money to assist the slaves were called "stockholders."

6. The escaped slaves were called "freight or cargo."

7. Abolitionists were people who spoke out against slavery and wanted it stopped.

Routes Taken by Escaped Slaves

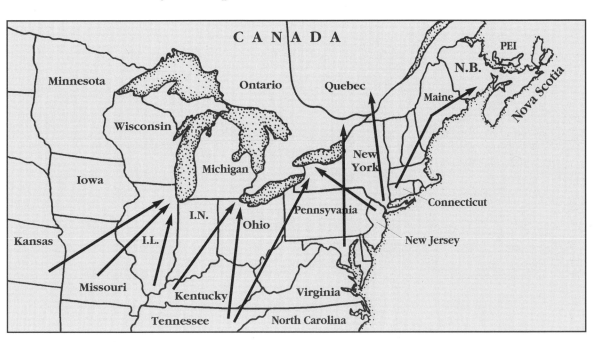

25

Activity 10: Freedom Train Quiz

The answers to these questions are in this book, but to find all the answers you may have to read ahead a few pages. See how many you can get.

1. Where did the slaves escape from? _____

2. People who spoke out against slavery and helped slaves to freedom were called

    _____.

3. What continent did the slaves come from originally? _____

4. When did slavery end in Canada? _____

5. Two newspapers were published to help Blacks who had escaped slavery. They were called

    _____ and the _____.

6. For how long did the Underground Railroad run?_____

7. Escaped slaves from the United States came to Canada before slavery ended here. Why?

   _____

8. A famous female Underground Railroad conductor was _____.

9. Name a place where escaped slaves settled._____.

10. A popular novel written in 1852 made many people aware of the hardships that slaves suffered and of their efforts to escape. What was the name of the book?

   _____

11. Name an event before 1840 that bought former slaves from the United States to Canada.

   _____

12. A community was set up near Chatham, Ontario, where Blacks could settle and live. What was its name?

   _____

How did you do?

Turn to page 60 and check your answers.
Give yourself 1 point for each correctly answered question.

10 to 12 points— Wow! Super job! Harriet would be proud of you.
7 to 9 points— Hey! Not bad.
Less than 7 points— We know you can do better!
                         Keep trying and keep learning.

Josiah Henson (1789-1883)

Despite years of cruelty, Josiah Henson tried hard to serve the men he worked for. But in return for his loyalty, he was cheated out of money he had saved to buy his freedom. In 1830 when a slave-owner tried to separate him from his family and sell him, he escaped to Canada with his wife and children.

Henson played a very important role in helping other Blacks. He returned to the United States to lead them to freedom and helped them settle in Canada. A Methodist minister, one of Henson's accomplishments was to help create the Dawn Settlement near Chatham, Ontario, a place where Blacks could study and live. Henson's life was recorded in a book called *The Life of Josiah Henson, Formally a Slave, Now an Inhabitant of Canada*. It is from this book, many believe, that American author Harriet Beecher Stowe got the idea for her popular novel *Uncle Tom's Cabin*.

Thousands of readers became aware of the terrible lives that slaves endured and of their efforts to escape.

Henson's teaching to other Blacks stressed the importance of owning their own land and growing a variety of products. This, he believed, would give meaning to their lives.

Activity 11: Underground Railroad Maze

You are a conductor on the Undergound Railroad. Can you lead your cargo to freedom? Your journey will be long and hard. Don't lose your path, and watch out for bounty hunters!
Additional questions found on page 56.

FREEDOM
Look Out! Bounty hunters!
Turn Back! Bloodhounds!
Watch It! Run and Hide!
Look Out! Bounty hunters!
Danger! Wild Animals!
Go Back! Dead End!
Jump over the page number!

Medicine

Dr. Anderson Ruffin Abbott (1837-1913)

Dr. Anderson Ruffin Abbott was the first Black born in Canada (1837) to become a doctor. Graduating from the Toronto School of Medicine in 1857, he served as one of eight Black surgeons for the Union Army during the American Civil War. He reached the position of Chief Medical Officer for Camp Baker and Freedman's Hospitals near Washington. Even though the war was about ending slavery, the white officers in the Union Army still did not want the troops mixed together. This sometimes made it difficult for him to receive all the equipment he needed.

After the death of President Abraham Lincoln, Mrs. Lincoln presented Abbott with a plaid shawl President Lincoln wore on his way to his inauguration. It formed part of a disguise some say the president wore on that occasion to escape assassination.

Elijah McCoy (1843-1929)

Elijah McCoy was an inventor who was fascinated by steam engines. As a mechanic in the early 1870s he noticed that machines had to be stopped every time they needed oil, which wasted a lot of time and was expensive. McCoy invented a device to oil the machinery while it was working. It was soon used on engines and train locomotives, on Great Lakes steamships, on ocean liners, and on machinery in factories.

His invention became so popular that no engine or machine was considered complete until it had a McCoy Lubricator. The phrase "real McCoy" soon caught on as a way of saying that people were getting the very best equipment available.

Elijah McCoy was born in 1843 in Colchester, Ontario. His parents had escaped slavery in Kentucky by using the Underground Railroad. At age 15 he was sent to Scotland to study engineering. But when he returned to Canada, the only job he could get was as a railway fireman (the person who put wood into the furnace). It was during this time that his mind started to look for better ways to do things.

By 1923 McCoy was known throughout the world. His inventions were patented in Great Britain, France, Germany, Austria, and Russia as well as in Canada and the United States. His work as an inventor came during a time that was very difficult for Black people; yet, through hard work he succeeded and made a great contribution.

Activity 12: Build a Traffic Light

The traffic light was developed by another famous Black inventor, Garret A. Morgan. Follow the directions and make your own working model. You will need an adult to help you. Additional questions found on page 58.

Things you'll need for this project:

- An empty 2 litre milk carton (the large size)
- Construction paper
- Thin cardboard
- Red, yellow and green tissue paper
- Transparent tape
- Paper glue
- Two "build 'em up" paper fasteners (available at stationery stores)
- A small glass with a round rim, 5 cm (2") in diameter
- A pencil
- An x-acto knife or any knife with a small, very sharp blade
- Scissors
- A skewer
- A flashlight

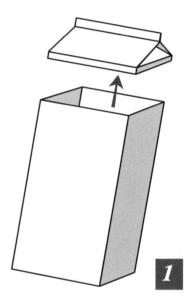

1. Ask an adult to cut the pouring spout end off the milk carton with the knife. Wash and dry the inside of the carton.

2. Cover the outside of the carton with construction paper and tape in place. Be sure to leave the cut end of the carton open.
Most traffic lights are either black or bright yellow, but you can use any colour of paper you like. You could even use leftover gift wrap.

3. Choose one side of the carton where there's no paper seams or tape showing. This will be the front of your traffic light.

Draw three circles on the front of the carton by tracing around the rim of the glass with the pencil. The first circle should be 1.5 cm (1/2") from the bottom of the carton. There should be 1.5 cm (1/2") between each circle. Ask an adult to cut the circles out of the carton with the knife.

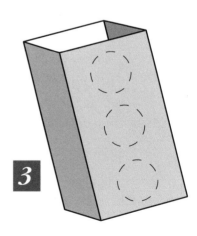

4. Now make the light covers:

Cut two 7 cm (2 3/4") squares out of the same paper you used to cover the carton. Cut two more rectangles the same size out of the thin cardboard. Paste the paper rectangles on top of the cardboard ones.

32

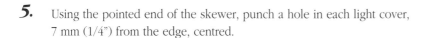

5. Using the pointed end of the skewer, punch a hole in each light cover, 7 mm (1/4") from the edge, centred.

6. Punch two holes in the front of the carton, centring each hole between the circles as shown.

Attach the light covers to the carton with the paper fasteners. (You will probably have to skewer the holes several times to make them large enough for the paper fasteners to fit. The holes should be large enough to allow the light covers to rotate.)

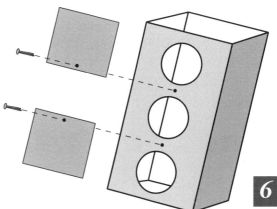

6

7. Now colour the lights:
Cut three 7 cm (2 3/4") squares of tissue paper, a red, a yellow and a green one.

Tape the tissue paper squares over the circles <u>inside</u> the carton. Be sure to put the red square over the circle closest to the bottom of the carton (which is the top of the traffic light). The yellow light is in the middle and the green is at the end.

You are now ready to direct traffic!
Hold your traffic light with the cut end down, and shine the flashlight up through it. If all systems are GO, spin the light covers around to hide the red and yellow circles, and you'll be giving the green light!

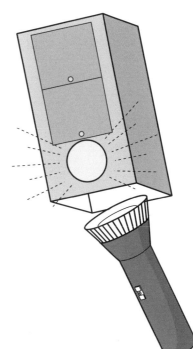

Marcus Garvey (1887-1940)

One of the first true national leaders in pursuit of civil rights for Black people was Marcus Garvey. Jamaican born, he came to Canada from the United States in 1928 after starting the Universal Negro Improvement Association (UNIA). It was the first group designed to unite Blacks all over the world. Garvey wanted Blacks to be proud of themselves and their origins. He saw this as the first step towards equality.

A gifted public speaker, he spent a great deal of time going throughout the country and spreading his message. Famous for saying that he wanted Blacks to be "the best Black person not the worst white person," Garvey opened the eyes of a generation of people.

His wife Amy is credited with keeping UNIA going, particularly during a time when, because of his activities, he was put in prison in the United States. With her help he became an important role model. His influence was later seen and heard in the words and actions of important black leaders like Martin Luther King, Jr., and Malcolm X.

Activity 13: Colour the Flag— Unity

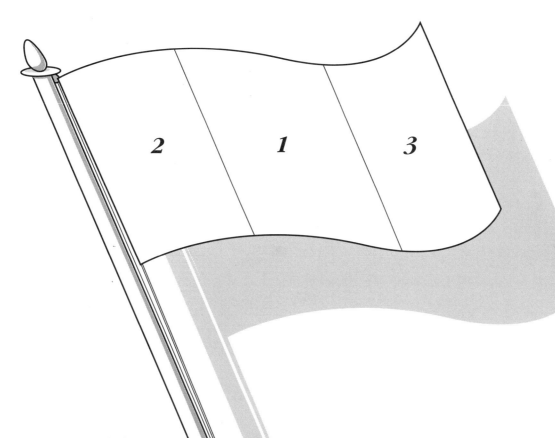

The colours associated with the
Black Flag of Unity are:
1. Black   2. Red   3. Green

Colour the flag according to the
number on each panel. Each of the
colours has a special meaning.
They are:
1. Black— people
2. Red— struggle
3. Green— earth

Another important colour is yellow
which means hope.

Mifflin Gibbs (*ca* 1840-1880)

Mifflin Gibbs was one of Victoria's most important citizens in the 1800s. He was the first Black elected to city council. Gibbs was an educated man who knew a great deal about the history of Black people and became a natural leader in the community. Gibbs also played role in British Colombia's becoming a part of Canada in 1871.

Alfred Shadd (1870-1915)

Alfred Shadd was the first Black to run in a provincial election. In 1901 he tried but failed in his attempt to get elected as a Conservative Member in the assembly of the North-West Territories. A few years later when a portion of the territories became the province of Saskatchewan he again tried for political office. He was again defeated, but this time the margin was just 52 votes. Shadd went on to become a highly respected doctor and community member in central Saskatchewan.

William Hubbard (1842-1945)

William Hubbard was a well-known politician in Toronto at the turn of the century. He served as alderman from 1894 to 1907, winning 13 annual elections in a row. He was elected again in 1913.

   The son of a Virginia refugee, he worked as a livery man in his uncle's business during his early years. He trained as a baker and eventually formed his own company, Hubbard Ovens, to sell an oven he invented.

   A gifted speaker, Hubbard also was prominent on the Toronto Board of Control and became its vice chairman. He was second in rank only to the mayor whom he often stood in for.

Activity 14: Other Flags of the World

Follow the instructions to draw some other famous flags.

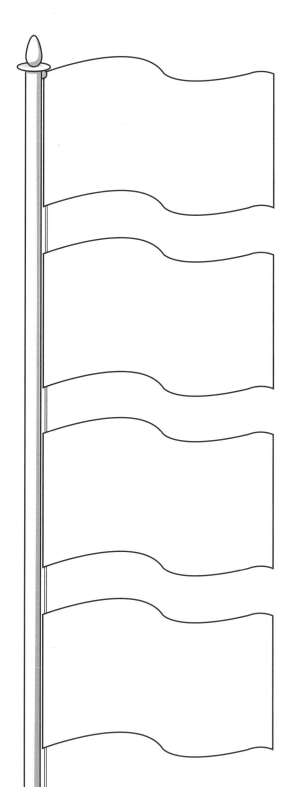

Canada

The flag of Canada is in two colours:
- two red bands at either side
- a white central section

There is a red maple leaf in the centre with 11 points, representing the 10 provinces and the territories.

Senegal

The flag of the African country of Senegal is in three colours:
- a green band on the inside, closest to the flagpole
- a yellow band in the middle
- A red band on the outside

There is a green star in the middle of the yellow section.

United Kingdom

This three-colour flag, called the Union Jack, is made up of three different crosses in red, white and blue:
- On a blue background, a wide diagonal cross in white goes from the top left-hand corner to the bottom right-hand corner, and from the top right-hand corner to the bottom left-hand corner.
- A red line covers the white cross, with a white margin on each side.
- Over the diagonal cross goes a wide white cross, with a narrower red cross in the centre.

United States of America

The flag of the United Ststes is made up of three colours: red, white and blue:
- A blue square in the top left-hand corner contains 50 white stars for the 50 states.
- The rest of the flag is made up of alternating red and white stripes.

Activity 15: Design Your Own Country's Flag

You have been named Prime Minister of your own country. What would your flag look like and why?

Rose Fortune
(ca 1774-1865)

In 1783 Rose Fortune became Canada's first policewoman, working in the port of Annapolis Royal, Nova Scotia. She was an independent woman, who went into business on her own as a baggage handler, meeting the boats from Boston and Saint John. Her duties also included pushing the loads of trunks, boxes, and carpet bags from the wharf to homes and hotels. As the town grew she became the police department of Annapolis Royal, keeping order on the wharf. Her special responsibility was to walk with important people to the dock so they would arrive safely and on time to catch their boats.

The Victoria Pioneer
Rifle Company

Also called the African Rifles, the Victoria Pioneer Rifle Company was formed in 1860 as a result of the growing Black population in Victoria, British Columbia. Originally a militia unit it took on policing duties and for some time was the only organized defence force in Victoria. Racism and jealousy took their toll however, and the Rifles encountered resistance to their continued existence.

Entertainment

Portia White (1911-1968)

Portia White was born in the town of Truro, Nova Scotia. She made her musical debut at the age of six in her father's church choir. At the age of 17, while teaching school she received her first break, winning a silver cup in the Nova Scotia Music Festival. From this experience she then had the good fortune to receive a scholarship from the Halifax Ladies Music Club so she could attend the Halifax Conservatory of Music. The Nova Scotia government recognized her talent and assisted her by establishing the Nova Scotia Talent Trust to aid her training. After making successful debuts in Toronto and New York she began touring over the world and became an important musical ambassador for our country.

One of the highlights of her career was singing for Queen Elizabeth at the opening of the Confederation Centre in Charlottetown, P.E.I. in 1964.

Activity 16: Get the Story

You are a newspaper reporter. After reading the story of Portia White, look around your community and write a headline and story for your paper on somebody you think is important. Share your first draft with a friend and use some of their ideas to improve your newspaper.

Remember to answer the five w's: **Who, What, Where, When** and **Why**.
Draw a picture of the person in the space provided.

THE FREE PRESS

Your Newspaper

Harry Jerome (1940-1983)

One of Canada's most outstanding athletes, Harry Jerome won a bronze medal at the 1964 Tokyo Olympics. At the Commonwealth Games in 1966, he won the gold medal and secured his place as one of the world's top sprinters. His success and the other contributions he made to sport in Canada earned him the Order of Canada, a medal given to honour our finest citizens. Harry Jerome was born in Saskatchewan but called British Columbia home for much of his life. He was named British Columbia's Athlete of the Century.

After his death in 1982, the Harry Jerome Society was formed to keep his memory alive and to make people aware and take pride in their Canadian heroes. One of his wishes was for Black children to strive for excellence in everything they do.

George Dixon (1870-1909)

George Dixon was born in Africville, Nova Scotia (a community just outside Halifax) in 1870. He began his boxing career at the age of 16. He was the first boxer to win three world championships in different weight classes. Fighting out of Boston, he held the title in the paperweight, bantamweight, and featherweight divisions. He once fought in a bout that lasted four hours, 40 minutes and eventually ended in a tie. Recognized for his great speed he is credited with inventing shadow boxing as a method of training.

Dixon fought in about 130 bouts and had more than 30 title defences. A recreation centre in Halifax is named in his honour.

Sam Langford (1886-1956)

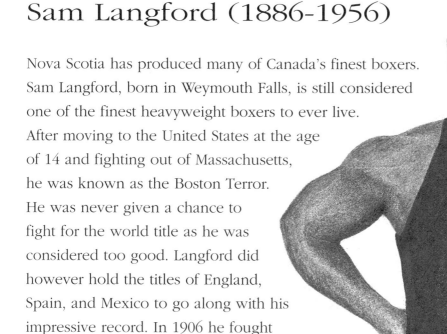

Nova Scotia has produced many of Canada's finest boxers. Sam Langford, born in Weymouth Falls, is still considered one of the finest heavyweight boxers to ever live. After moving to the United States at the age of 14 and fighting out of Massachusetts, he was known as the Boston Terror. He was never given a chance to fight for the world title as he was considered too good. Langford did however hold the titles of England, Spain, and Mexico to go along with his impressive record. In 1906 he fought American Jack Johnson who shortly thereafter became the first Black to hold the title of World Heavyweight Champion.

Activity 17: Great Canadian Athletes (Past and Present)

From the information given can name these African Canadian athletes? Can you can find out more about them? Describe which clues you used to find out the answer and write about your search.

1. M _ _ _ _ _ _ _   T _ _ _ _ _   B _ _ _ _ _

From Lockeport, Nova Scotia, she was a member of Canada's Olympic track and field teams in 1964, 1968, and 1972. She won a silver medal at the 1978 Commonwealth Games held in Edmonton and held four Canadian records during her sprinting career.

2. W _ _ _ _ _   _'_ _ _

This native of Fredericton, New Brunswick was called the Jackie Robinson of hockey. He was the first Black to play in the National Hockey League when he took to the ice with the Boston Bruins in 1958 at the Montreal Forum in a game against the Canadians.

3. _ _ _ _ _ _ _ _   J _ _ _ _ _ _

One of the best pitchers of all time, he played for 19 years in the major leagues. During that time he won a Cy Young award as the best pitcher in the National League. He is the only Canadian player to be selected for the Baseball Hall of Fame in Cooperstown, New York.

4. S _ _ _ _ _   S _ _ _ _ _ _

She was a member of Canada's National and Olympic basketball teams and took part in the 1976, 1980, and 1984 Olympic Games. Since her athletic career ended she has gone on to become an award-winning newsperson and most recently a filmmaker.

5. _ _ _ _ _   D _ _ _

He was introduced to boxing in 1953 by accident when he took the place of an absent fighter. He went on to win the contest with a knockout. With his record of 81 wins in 88 bouts, he became a very important role model to many young Canadian boxers. He is currently the Sergeant at Arms for the Province of Nova Scotia.

6. _ _ _ _   F _ _

He is one of only a few Canadians ever to play in the National Basketball Association. He is currently a member of the Boston Celtics, one of the most famous sports teams in the world.

7. G _ _ _ _   _ _ _ _

He is regarded by many as one of the finest goaltenders of all time. He was a key figure in the Edmonton Oilers' climb to the top of the National Hockey League. He has played in four Stanley Cup championships and has also represented Canada as a member of Team Canada in world championships and Canada Cup play.

8. J _ _ _ _   B _ _ _ _ _

As a teenager she won the both the junior and senior women's table tennis championships in 1988. She has been a member of Canada's national teams, competing in the Commonwealth Games and World Championships.

Family

Activity 18: This Is Us

Fill in the information below for each member of your family. If you can, include grandparents and aunts and uncles along with your parents and brothers and sisters. Additional questions found on page 58.

NAME	AGE	MY FAVOURITE:				
		COLOUR	FOOD	HOBBY	BOOK	TV SHOW

Put yourself here.

Activity 19: Discover Your Roots

Write in the names of your family members to complete this family tree. For each person, write down a special achievement or something that they are famous for—in your family or in your community. Maybe your brother can whistle any tune he's ever heard, or your grandmother won a special award. Ask your parents for help if you need it.

Activity 20: Kente Pattern

The brightly coloured cloth worn by many African Canadians to give recognition to their past is called Kente (ken-tee). It can come in many patterns and is thought to originate from a time when there were kings and queens in many countries of Africa. Kente serves much the same purpose as the tartan does for Scottish people— to show family connection.

Here are three samples of Kente patterns.

  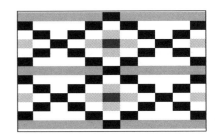

Design your own kente pattern, using the grid below; then colour your kente. Remember the special meanings for colours on page 35. Are there any colours that make you happy or have special meaning for you? You can use them in your kente.

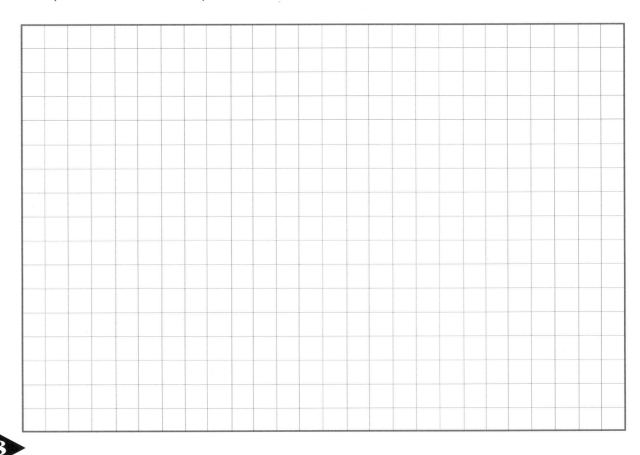

Additional questions found on page 58.

When Black and White See Eye to Eye

When Black and White see eye-to-eye
Good times go round and round
But when they don't
Some push, some shout
Some fight; all stand and frown.

See eye-to-eye, I always say
See hand-to-hand
See heart-to-heart
See mind to mind to mind
Then Black meets White
Meets Brown meets Tan
Meets French meets Mi'kmaq
Meets Arab meets Jew
When Black and White see eye-to-eye
This world fits and pleases me and you.

—*Maxine Tynes*

If you see truth

If you hear a lie
pass it by
If you see truth
spread it far and wide

—*Lillian Allen*

49

Activity 21: Famous Black Role Models

Match the names and achievements of these famous Black celebrities by putting the correct number in each blank.

A. Muhammed Ali	1. Lieutenant-Governor	A _____
B. Dr. Carrie Best	2. Athlete	B _____
C. Maya Angelou	3. Entertainer	C _____
D. Oscar Peterson	4. Civil rights leader	D _____
E. Oprah Winfrey	5. Poet/writer	E _____
F. Lincoln Alexander	6. Musician/composer	F _____
G. Martin Luther King	7. Community leader	G _____
H. Rosemary Brown	8. Politician	H _____

2. Find out more about one of these people and make a report to the class.

3. Design an award to be presented to the person for his or her achievement.

4. Write a letter to the person, inviting him or her to your community. Tell why you think your community would be a good place to visit.

5. Write a poem about the person you have chosen or about how you feel when you have done something special.

Activity 22: People— Past and Present

Match the letters with the numbers to reveal the names of famous Black people from history and the present day.

A — 1
B — 2
C — 3
D — 4
E — 5
F — 6
G — 7
H — 8
I — 9
J — 10
K— 11
L — 12
M — 13
N — 14
O — 15
P — 16
Q — 17
R — 18
S — 19
T — 20
U — 21
V — 22
W — 23
X — 24
Y — 25
Z — 26

1. __ __ __ __ __ __ __ __
    13 1 12 3 15 12 13   24

2. __ __ __ __ __ __ __ __ __ __ __ __
    14 5 12 19 15 14   13 1 14 4 5 12 1

3. __ __ __ __ __ __ __ __ __
    3 12 5 15 16 1 20 18 1

4. __ __ __ __ __ __ __ __ __ __ __ __ __ __
    17 21 5 5 14   3 8 1 18 12 15 20 20 5

    __ __ __ __ __ __
    19 15 16 8 9 1

5. __ __ __ __ __ __ __ __ __ __ __ __ __ __
    1 12 5 24 1 14 4 18 5   4 21 13 1 19

6. __ __ __ __ __
    1 5 19 15 16

7. __ __ __ __ __ __ __ __
    8 1 14 14 9 2 1 12

8. __ __ __ __ __ __
    14 26 9 14 7 1

Try to find out more about each person. Write a report on one of them.

51

We are the future

We are lovers of the earth
who wish for peace
We are keepers of the soul
who fight for human rights
We are the sons and daughters
who must make wrongs right
We are the future
who stand up for our rights

—*Lillian Allen*

Glossary of Terms

African Canadian – Citizen of Canada of African descent

Africville – An African Canadian community near Halifax, Nova Scotia whose residents were forced off their land during the 1960's to enable the City of Halifax to build a bridge

Ancestor – A member of the same family who lived very long ago

Assassination – To murder by secret or sudden attack

Black Loyalists — Name given to Black refugees who fled to Canada after the American Revolution in 1776

Bounty hunter — Someone who hunts another person for the sake of reward

Cavalry – Part of an army that fights on horseback

Congregation – A gathering; especially a group of people belonging to a church

Debut – The first public appearance of a performer

Discrimination – To make a difference in treatment or favour someone on a basis other than merit

Doctrine – A set of beliefs

Editor – The person who decides what stories will appear in a newspaper

Inauguration – The ceremony used to swear in a new president (United States of America)

Latitude – Position on the globe north or south of the equator. The border between Canada and the United States from Manitoba to British Columbia runs along the 49th parallel (49°N)

Lecture – A talk about a subject given to a class or other audience

Livery man – Person who works in a stable where horses and vehicles are hired (rented)

Longitude – Position on the globe east or west of Greenwich, England. The capital of Canada, Ottawa, is located at 75°W

Mi'kmaq – A group of Native people living in Atlantic Canada

Moses – Name given to Harriet Tubman, because she acted in much the same manner as Moses did when he led the people of Israel to freedom

Patent – A document giving an inventor the right to be the only person who can make, use, or sell an invention

Racism – A belief that one race is superior to another

Regiment – A military unit consisting of a number of smaller units called battalions

Rodeo – A public performance featuring bronco riding, calf roping, steer wrestling, and bull riding

Segregate – To separate or set apart from others

Slave – A human being whose freedom has been stolen and who is owned by another. Slaves were bought and sold, often separating children from their parents. They had to do whatever work they were told to do. If they tried to escape they were punished severely

U N I A – United Negro Improvement Association, group founded by Marcus Garvey

Victoria Cross – Highest medal of honour given in the British Commonwealth for bravery in battle, named for Queen Victoria

The Black Cultural Centre for Nova Scotia

The Black Cultural Centre for Nova Scotia opened in September 1983. Built by the Black Cultural Society in its effort to preserve, protect, and promote Black culture in Nova Scotia and around the world, it consists of a museum, library, amphitheatre, and gift shop.

Programs of the Black Cultural Centre for Nova Scotia extend beyond its doors to the broader community of Nova Scotia. These efforts are achieved through workshops, seminars, school and community presentations.

The Black Cultural Centre has also published a number of books, including histories, poetry, drama, and fiction. These books are written by and about Nova Scotians.

The Black Cultural Centre for Nova Scotia has become one of Canada's leading resource and information sites dealing with Black experience in Canada. In its efforts to increase the archives, interested persons are asked to donate any pictures or information they might have. Proper recording, documentation, and safekeeping of Black history is vital if it is to be passed on to future generations.

Membership and other information can be obtained by contacting:

The Black Cultural Centre for Nova Scotia   (902) 434–6223
1149 Main Street   (902) 434–2306 (fax)
Dartmouth, Nova Scotia B2Z 1A8   1–800–465–0767 (toll free)

Congress of Black Women

The Congress of Black Women is a national organization with chapters across Canada. It began in 1973 when more than 300 women met to discuss issues that concerned everyone, such as racism, education, and human rights.

When it became officially organized, the goal of having stronger links between Black women of African, Caribbean, American, or Canadian backgrounds was seen as a priority.

In recent years it has become a national leader in the awareness and promotion of important women's issues such as health care and the value of education and its role in society.

Ontario Black History Society

The Ontario Black History Society was started in 1978 by a small group of dedicated individuals as a result of questions that arose from many different people who wished to study and discuss African Canadian history.

One of the first activities of the society was to celebrate Black History Week in February 1979. The society marked the occasion with the unveiling of a portrait of William Hubbard, the politician who played a prominent role in Toronto during the early 1900s.

The society has also co-operated with the Bicentennial Black Heritage Committee to produce a presentation entitled *Hallelujah, Ont.*, which traces the 200-year-old history of Black contribution in the province.

Now located at the Ontario Heritage Centre in Toronto, the organization serves a role as a necessary cultural and educational resource.

Reading Material

There is a growing selection of reading and reference material dealing with African Canadians and people of African descent all over the world. The following is a short list of selected books that will help you to continue your search for information.

Davison, Basil, and the Editors of Time-Life Books. *African Kingdoms*. Amsterdam: Time-Life Books, 1966 and reprinted 1984.

Ellis, Veronica Freeman. *Afro Bets: First Book About Africa*. New Jersey: Just Us Books, 1989.

Grunsell, Angela. *Let's Talk About Racism*. New York: Gloucester Press, 1991.

Hacker, Carlotta. *Bravery*. Ontario: Fitzhenry and Whiteside, Ltd., 1989.

Halliburton, Warren J. *Celebrations of African Heritage*. New York: Crestwood House, 1992.

Haskins, Jim, and Kathleen Benson. *Space Challenger: The Story of Gulon Bluford*. Minneapolis: Carolrhoda Books Inc., 1984.

Hill, Daniel G. *The Freedom Seekers: Blacks in Early Canada*. Toronto: Stoddart, 1991.

Hill, Lawrence. *Trials and Triumphs: The Story of African Canadians*. Toronto: Umbrella Press, 1993.

Kunjufu, Jawanza. *Lessons In History: A Celebration In Blackness*. (Elementary edition) Chicago: African American Images, 1987.

Lind, Jane. *The Underground Railroad*. Toronto: Grolier Limited, 1990.

Lowery, Linda. *Martin Luther King Day*. Minneapolis: Carolahoda Books, 1987.

Musgrove, Margaret. *Ashanti To Zulu*. Dillon, Leo and Diane, illustrators. Wing King Tong Company, 1976.

Tolan, Mary, and Susan Taylor-Boyd. *People Who Made A Difference: Sojourner Truth*. Garth Stevens Children's Books, 1991.

Winter, Jeanette. *Follow the Drinking Gourd*. Books for Young Readers, 1992.

Additional Activities

Activity 1a

1. Find the continent of Africa on a globe or a map of the world.
2. Find the southern-most country on the continent of Africa. What is the latitude and longitude of the capital city?
3. A large group of people living in this country were once led by a great king. Find out the name of the people and the name of this famous leader.

Activity 2a

1. Design and create your own hieroglyphs using things around you.
2. Write a secret hieroglyphic message to a friend using your code. See if they can figure it out without the code.

Activity 6a

Port Royal and Sierra Leone are important historical settlement areas. Choose one and write a report on why it was so important. Is this place still in existence today?

Activity 9a

1. Find out more about stained glass windows, for example, how they are made?
2. Design your own stained glass picture with a message that is important to you.
3. Is there any stained glass in your community? If there is, investigate its history.

Activity 10a

1. Go to the map on page 25 and choose one of the routes to freedom taken by escaped slaves. Working from a map in an atlas, describe the journey. The map scale and colours will help you. How far is the journey? What towns or cities do you pass? Do you have to cross any rivers? Is the route flat or hilly?
2. People of a certain religion were helpful to escaping slaves. (a) Who were they? (b) Why and how were they helpful?
3. Many books, both fiction and non-fiction, have been written about this time period (1861- 65). Ask a librarian to help you find one of these books, read it, and make a report to your parents or class on what you have read.

Activity 11a

In the grid below, design your own escape maze. Write about some of the dangers that might happen along the way.

Activity 12a

Many discoveries and inventions have come about because people like Elijah McCoy thought of ways to do their work better or make their lives easier. (a) Describe an invention that would help you or someone you know (b) draw a picture of it, and tell how you would make it.

Activity 18a

1. Write a report on preferences between males and females, in the following areas: colour, food, and hobbies.
2. Share your information with other children and make a chart showing how males and females and people of different ages have different preferences.

Activity 20a

Kente patterns are often compared to Scottish tartans because they show that the person who is wearing one belongs to a certain family or clan.

Find out more about tartans. Does your family have a tartan or a kente? Draw it, or design a tartan or kente for your family. Tell why you have chosen this design.

Answers

Activity 1 page 3 The continent is AFRICA.

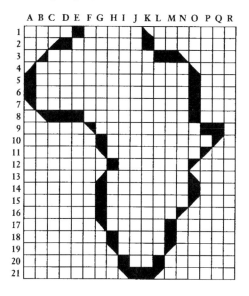

Activity 1a page 3

Pretoria is located at latitude 25°S; longitude 28°E. Shaka was the King of the Zulu tribe in the years 1818 to 1828.

Activity 2 page 5

I WOULD NEVER BE OF ANY SERVICE TO ANYONE AS A SLAVE.   —NAT TURNER

Activity 3 page 7

Here are some other questions that an interviewer might ask the first person to visit Canada:

6. What did you see?
7. Did you meet anyone while travelling?
8. Was there anything you didn't like about Canada?
9. Was Canada your first choice as a place to go?
10. If you could take something good from Canada, what would it be?
11. Is Canada the kind of country you would recommend to other visitors? Why?

Activity 4, page 11

Here are some examples: blanket, food, clothes, socks, map, matches, water bottle, axe, gun, gun powder, bullets, fishing line, fish hooks, cooking pot, seeds to grow things, bible

Activity 5, page 13

1. The medal was first given in 1856. In 1972 it was replaced in Canada by Canadian bravery awards.
2. The medal was named for Queen Victoria who ruled from 1837-1901.
3. In all, 93 Canadians were awarded the Victoria Cross.
4. The head of the Commonwealth— the Queen (or King) of England— gives this award.
5. The capital of British Columbia is also named after Queen Victoria.

Activity 6, page 15

1. Asia
2. Dover, Mary, Ann
3. Victory
4. Halifax
5. Inkerman, Sebastopol
6. Port Royal
7. Sierra Leone

Activity 8, page 21

Solution: HE WAS A REALLY COOL DUDE.

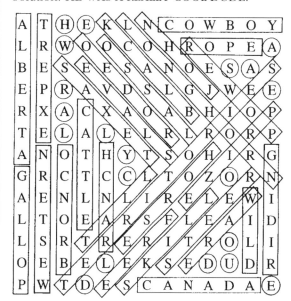

Activity 9, page 23

Solution:

H
O
P
E

Activity 11, page 29

FREEDOM

Activity 10, page 26

1. The slaves escaped from the southern United States. Many were made to work on large farms called plantations.
2. Abolitionists
3. Africa
4. Slavery ended in 1834.
5. *Provincial Freeman* and *Voice of the Fugitive*
6. 1840 to 1860
7. After 1793 Canada refused to send escaped slaves back to the United States.
8. Harriet Tubman
9. Nova Scotia, Ontario, British Columbia
10. *Uncle Tom's Cabin* by Harriet Beecher Stowe
11. War of 1812
12. The Dawn Settlement

Activity 17, page 44

1. Marjorie Turner Bailey
2. Willie O'Ree
3. Ferguson Jenkins
4. Sylvia Sweeney
5. Buddy Daye
6. Rick Fox
7. Grant Fuhr
8. Julie Barton

Activity 21, page 50

A 2
B 7
C 5
D 6
E 3
F 8
G 4
H 1

Activity 22, page 51

1. Malcolm X
2. Nelson Mandela
3. Cleopatra
4. Queen Charlotte Sophia
5. Alexandre Dumas
6. Aesop
7. Hannibal
8. Nzinga

Activity 14, page 37

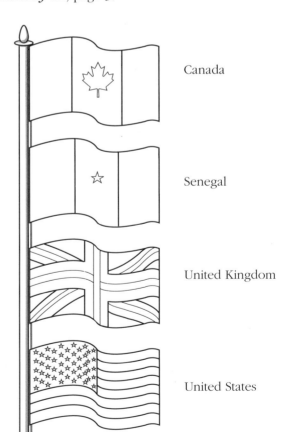

Canada

Senegal

United Kingdom

United States